HABITATS

ALSO BY KATHARINE WHITCOMB

The Daughter's Almanac

Saints of South Dakota and Other Poems

CHAPBOOKS

Hosannas

Lamp of Letters

NONFICTION

The Art Courage Program
(with Brian Goeltzenleuchter)

HABITATS

poems

KATHARINE WHITCOMB

Everett • Seattle
Washington

Copyright © 2024 by Katharine Whitcomb

All rights reserved
Printed in the United States of America
First Edition

Cover design by Kathleen Lynch/Black Kat Design
Book design by Abi Pollokoff

Poetry NW Editions is an independent, non-profit educational press in residence at Everett Community College.

Library of Congress Control Number: 2023951428
Names: Whitcomb, Katharine, author
Title: Habitats / Katharine Whitcomb
Description: First Edition / Everett, Washington: Poetry NW Editions, 2024
ISBN-13: 978-1-949166-08-8

Poetry NW Editions
2000 Tower Street
Everett, Washington 98201

www.poetrynw.org

This book is for my father, Richard Owens Whitcomb,
1926-2020,
with all my love and gratitude.

Il me manque profondément, et chaque jour,
sa présence m'accompagne.

CONTENTS

I. FOREST

Sleepless Ode	3
Lines for Mid-Winter	4
Losers	5
Mercy	7
Thrush-Wife	9
Murder Mystery	10
Octaves of Stubborn Devotion	11
Winter Weather	13
Flame in a Jar	14
Crossing to Friday Harbor	15
The Bird	17
Winter Saturday	19
Memory	20

II. HOTELS

Sestina of Human Longing	23
Hotel Vienna	25
Habitat	26
Along the Narrow Road Some Sunlight	27
Remembering Paris	28
Hotel Ljubljana	29
Hotel Box with Vermeer Detail, Joseph Cornell, 1955	30
Hotel Santa Maria	31
Villa Romana Balaca	32
Hotel Istanbul	33
No Reservations	35
I Think of God in the Turbulence	37
Hotel Budapest	39

After Reading Bashō, I Remember the Rain	41
Waltham Field Station	43
Hotel Poem	45

III. DREAMS

Meaning All Meaning Ending Here	49
Augury	50
Greenland, 1350	51
Pratzen Hill	52
Inscription Found on a Cliff Face After Drought	53
Snowberry in Drought Season	54
Trail	56
Animate Objects	58
Love Poem for Anna Karenina	59
Cypher	61
National Zoo, January 6, 2021	62
Number Spell to Change Your Luck	63
Daily, Under My Breath	64
Not Today	66
I Keep the Calendar Alive	67
After Apple-Picking	68
The Details	70
Poem for the Day the World Will End	71

Acknowledgments	73
With Gratitude	75
Notes on the Poems	77

Cornell was a gatherer, not an owner. He was also a builder of bowers, which he called "habitats," as befits someone who adored birds.

—Maggie Nelson

In my heart and its rooms is dark and windy.

—Deborah Digges

I. FOREST

Sleepless Ode

o lost person
            do you remember

reading a book in gray-green spring light
        yr back flat on the cab window of a borrowed pick-up
            eleven p.m. yr knees propping yr elbows
                & how we always headed north
        to Ontario to nearly vacant provincial
parks for aimless slow-houred weekends
& how a moose dripping w/ lake weed
        dozing on his feet in the middle of the camp road
            didn't care about us (awestruck us)
                I think of you now in spring
        again & I just want to sit outside
in an old wild empty place
wrapped in yr coat—as poor
        as we were poor then but there
            w/everything growing together awake
                & away from death all the livelong night

Lines for Mid-Winter

Time was we threw an annual solstice party to burn our burdens
—sent flaming tongue depressor boats downriver with a cargo of curling photos
of old boyfriends and bad habits scrawled on scraps.

We waved goodbye from the shore and made lists of good wishes.

This year I cannot do it. Instead, I stomp a big circle through the snow
a thousand footprints around the house and do not raise my face once,
though the birds overhead are hungry and I hear them.

For me, no more trying on shirts for a turn before the mirror; no
dreaming like a princess under my quilts.

I am not young or uncomplicated or down-to-earth.

The future is a candle-flame painted by Gerhard Richter.
The future is a lost dog on the road.

Inside my house a lamp is lit.
Through the window, the walnut bookcase
looks for a moment broad-shouldered and tall, like someone else.

Losers

I left my wallet on the back bumper of the Jetta
    after buying beer where it stayed
        for over 200 sketchy northern highway miles, burgundy
            leather lump intact.   My favorite
        Aimee Bender story describes an orphan who finds lost
    objects by concentrating on the tug of memory
awake in everything.   My friends say of course you
    like that one, because in the story trees remember
        where they were born and the lost boy is returned
            home unharmed.   Of course.   I used to dream that
        if I got too tired to drive a big god would reach
    into the car and carry me the rest of the way like a party-weary
toddler.   I wore my ex-husband's hat for years, a man's
    brimmed fedora, large on me, so that maybe for a while
        my cigarette-smoking alter-ego could think his thoughts.
                We would wait out the thunderstorms
        together in our bungalow's screened porch high above
    the Mississippi.   My father sometimes remembers
from his assisted living facility in Chicago his sisters
    are dead and the farm is long sold.   But I tell him
        not to fret.   Those things are not where we can
            find them, though we listen after them hard when they flash
        back up.   We lost Mom, we lost Maggie,
    too much, and kitchens, rings, gorgeous songs.
What happens to the bargain we make with each other—*you stay*
    alive while I am alive. If I am missing, please
        come find me.   By accident once I found myself down

                a wild grassed-over field-side road in Wisconsin
           with no one around and the wind whispering in
      collusion.   I can see that secret moment more
clearly than any face, as if that place might have
     offered me a choice I lost, like a garment or a life.

Mercy

Justin and I stole my boyfriend's Ford wagon
    for its beach pass sticker
and drove out to swim
      every good day without him.

Nobody was ever there but us
    on the cold, ocean-side beach. Black heads of seals
wobbled in the water a safe distance
      away from where we floated
facing skyward. Clouds crashed fast as racecars. We screamed
    over the roar about books we were reading,
which Beastie Boys songs we loved—
      bet who could outlast whom. The Atlantic
sighed gigantically from deep-lunged darkness.
    We needed jobs. Saltwater stung like burning jelly,
green laudanum, rubber band snaps on the wrist.

      Back in her Provincetown apartment our friend
Mary wanted to die but we did not know it
    as we swam like fetuses in cold alien wombs,
our brains slowing, ticking backward to zero.
      We could stand our bodies cradled there
with neither love nor comfort—the sea's harsh
    alacrity tazered fear until fear kept far from us.

Fuck the future.
      There is dumb mercy in the present moment,
before we part from each other forever,
    mercy in each minute of the senses' deft erasure.
We treaded water, shouting blue-lipped:
    you stay here stay here I dare you.

Thrush-Wife

        swallower of anger, swallow skimming above
      the creek, lark-flower, sorrow-
    wallower, frowner, furrowed-
brower, sleep-stalker

dust rustler, water-
    hater, worry-wart, daughter,
      warbler, thrasher, thrush-wife, ex-
        wife, dawn breaker, small high-gliding kite

Murder Mystery

So, the car rests side-saddle on the trail while she walks the dog
& she didn't tell anybody where she was going. No, no dog,

only her iPod but no purse or backpack, not even a PowerBar
in the pocket of her running pants. Or maybe the holidays

came & instead of flying east as usual she didn't but we just assumed.
The creek bubbles thickly over the rocks down the slope,

barely liquid. Footprints ink the snow but they're blown out.
No car, no dog, & the porch lights blaze all night & all day

in an un-notable way. No more piles of envelopes carried to
the post office, no sloppy shoveling jobs, no more shades up

then down, no gray garbage bin on the curb Sunday nights.
She kept a quiet house in the first place. Messages to the larger world

do not return the favor, she should have known. & fate has a tall swing
like the one out back, where once her feet hit the blue curtain of the sky.

Octaves of Stubborn Devotion

              I admit I mutter love to a half-needled
           straggly conifer shrub I named "Ugly-tree,"
    who persists through the winters & to drought-
starved creek irises too, who shrink browning
      in the run-off shallows. Hanging on. Harmed.
           Everything is so hungry. Forest fire smoke
                blazes months of sunsets. A raccoon pokes
garden dirt for grubs & worms.
                    Overnight
                              the small deaths. When I dream
                         they are my dreams, my lean &
                    stubborn devotions. I hear the gold
                finches burbling while my hands hold
                      my own head during dark afternoons. A slow-
                          blooming hibiscus hugs the wall. The field
                  I watch from the window was felled
                      of trees one hundred years ago.
              Now
forest covers ruined buildings
    & the dead sink to cover other dead things.
        I don't fix ripped-up chicken wire so now
            a skunk sleeps under the house. I know.
        I bought this house like I entered a marriage,
for the sound of the cottonwoods' chatter
            in late July, loud over ditchwater,
extravagant sighs in their language.
                  Oh

     how I love their enumerations & shy
    warnings. I lie awake wishing for fluency
   beyond myself. After my mother died
I let the yard go wild & quail nested
    under the sage bushes. Outside I feel air
      reverberating desperately around me
    as if in pity, like the bright green beetles
     who won't stop strafing my hair.

Winter Weather

      I used to walk a trail in the dunes
near Provincetown with my pockets full
      of birdseed. I liked the zip of the chickadees'

      scratchy feet on my hands
as they jockeyed for a spot. If I could feel them again, I
      might get in the spirit. No, these days

      out west I stop my car to call
over the horses from their grazing on Wilson Creek
      Road. The goats come sometimes

      to see if I have carrots.
I run out of things to say to humans, though I love them.
      Trash cans blow over in the wind

      by my house on the bare ground
this December. Unraked leaves will land somewhere else. Why
      did I come to rest here in this desert valley?

      What clues in the weather,
at the bottom of my cup? Air drags heavy clouds dark
      over the mountains. Let the world carry on:

      It's A Wonderful Life with helpful angels
and the wish for redemption. But I've grown tired of wishes,
      forgotten in a pocket, un-proffered.

Flame in a Jar

I dreamed I found a baby mouse in my water bottle and
    brought the sleeping tiny ball of fur
to someone for help: a boxer in a wool vest!
    He cupped the mouse in his palm   and heart fluttering
        I woke to the refrigerator hum of a dark house.

I sit bleary-eyed at my desk with coffee   and spy my cat
    stalking voles in the neighbor's yard.
He disappears after breakfast over the fence
    across the creek then turns up dirty at dinner.
        I once found him napping under a tree.

I don't think he is really a cat.   I had another dream
    about the souls of my dead pets though I'm not sure
what a soul is.   It was more that I saw them
    as people in a concentrated form—regal woman,
        shy orphan, tattooed skater punk.

I would know them if I saw them in a bus station
    or on my doorstep.   But what am I saying?
Is what makes a soul like a flame inside a jar?   Firefly, filament,
    bit of fur.   I woke worried, so weary,
        breathing hard and human.

Crossing to Friday Harbor

      No crowds on this ferry.
Not many faces looking into my face. I left my car by the others
         and climbed two flights of stairs

         to the passenger seats, beside
spray-splattered windows. I was not dreaming of my part in the great
         play. I too *lived*, with my fellow

         riders over the water. They
lolled, scattered over the hundred seats, feet up, phones to their ears.
         The sun was half an hour from darkness

         and the clouds hugged us
tightly. I could not listen to conversation; I descended back to
         the car deck where water was pounding.

         Gulls' bellies floated
at eye level over the air-wake and veered away. Behind the wheel
         I almost fell asleep to the roar of the boat engine.

         I too loved well some cities,
but far away, and some people, far away. I loved other ferries
         and other crossings to distant harbors.

         I try to find my way to disregard
what comes between us, any of us. I was cold there in my car,
         exhausted from traveling, fearful of Christmas'

sad memories in my blood—
so I thought of you, whose embrace of the human swings wider than
   death, who wrote *time or place—distance avails not.*

The Bird

       Outside the door of my rented cottage
lay a bird. As I heaved my book bag onto a chair he was there,
    close to the wall, beyond the sightline of the room.

       His body was so large the look of him
paralyzed me, orange, handsome orange, black with a bright beak.
    A foot and leg curled onto the cement, long

       feathers like a cape. Formal. Fluid
in a wet pool under his beak. The day blue at noon. Time stops
    with death. I could not do anything

       without first attending to him. I was not
prepared or brave. I found a bag, a big napkin and a glove.
    Stood over him, knelt on the rough deck,

       said *bird bird bird bird bird.*
I was afraid he was stunned, not moving; that he would try
    to fly and was not yet dead. I did not want

       to make it worse for him. But
when I leaned in over his white-ringed eye there was no flicker,
    gone. To touch him was not grave, but easy,

       light. I have no one
to give me advice on these things. I carried him across the green
    lawns to a dumpster. I wished then

more than ever for solitude.

Even the strangers inhabiting their quiet cottages were terrible.

And everything, everything, flocked around me.

Winter Saturday

      Last night I lay down
in front of the gas fireplace like an old dog
      and fell asleep on the rug.

      How long had it been,
what miles flown over full-speed, since sleep
      seeped in, warm as a drug?

      The day for once bore
no schisms, no battering-rammed doors leaned
      askew on their hooks.

      A forest carries quiet
like cloth in its arms. When I was a girl I dreamed
      this inside my books.

Memory

ticking out of her trance
for a moment
     the psychic's blue eyes shoot to mine
lucky! she snarls
       then blinks twice

(my heart on low like a gas burner
     forgotten   an open flame
guttering and dangerous
     in the empty house's embrace)

what an auspicious life
               she says
                   as if surprised
looking me up and down

     (a lizard on the roof high-
tails it to the chimney stack)

II. HOTELS

Sestina of Human Longing

I begin this poem with a bird singing a song
     that strikes my ear like the jangle a ring of keys
          makes slapping a janitor's hip, echo in memory,
  bird synching & dipping over the river, reader,
as I walk south of town. I am learning French
     through my headphones but I still hear the universe

          thrumming over the litany: *terre, planète, univers*.
    My language app uses game theory & little songs
play when I earn points. My avatar waves a French
     flag on the weekly scoreboard. Ask anyone, a key
          to fluency is consistency. At least I am good, reader,
at showing up, albeit virtually—in truth, the memory

of my trilingual parents guilts me into memorizing
     verb tenses: *partirai, partiras, partira*. I will leave a universe
          of questions unanswered when I go. For instance, reader,
  why isn't there ever enough time for poetry—those songs
in my youth, Plumly writing of rain the color of keys
     & Wright's "Homage to Paul Cezanne," praising a French

          painter with visions of the dead. I longed for France
    before I ever saw France & then after too. The memory
of Paris floats the city inside the city, old hotel room keys
     loose in coat pockets, lovers & husbands & a universe
          of loneliness but beautiful. It's like a favorite song
    that brings everything back. I know you know, reader,

I know you know. I like having you here, reading
    along patiently, traveling inside this stanza. French
        lessons make me humble, as does trying to sing
    anything. I have so many song lyrics memorized
& such a terrible voice. One of the basic rules of the universe,
    fortunately, is that nothing is perfect. This is a key

        premise from Stephen Hawking, (the locksmith!)
    who famously wrote *be brave, be curious*, reader,
& *be determined*. Can we know why the universe
    exists at all? I have put my hair up in a French
        twist & shrugged into an old dress. I remember
    walking to the river many times, same song

in my head, reader. The river rolls r's in French,
    aqua-throated, a universe of sound. Memory's
        strong, keys lost, pockets full of stones & songs.

Hotel Vienna

        now that no one loves me tiny angels
relinquish their architecture to circle my cheekbones
    their shields outstretched

    some surge through narrow alleys prickling the air
some whisper comfort into carriage horses' ears

        now that no one loves me angels sleep
on worn velvet sofas in Café Hawelka
    while coffee passes hand to hand above their heads

three bald angels arrange insects on a woman's shoulder
    stretching out each black spiny leg

    some extinguish the exit signs
        inside vast glowing museums

some smoke outside on the grand verandas

        now that no one loves me angels
unhook each precious painting
    to set the trees inside them free

        some bestow straw-and-flower garlands
    upon wool-suited matrons for me

without love here Nietzsche wrote *the world is deep*

Habitat

    To fit a washer/dryer into my small house
I pried accordion doors from a narrow hall
        closet & jammed them in so they protruded
menacingly into the passage.

In that weird space, arms braced against
     white enameled appliances, I bent screamng.

    I had just returned home from living abroad
for months with a man who did not love me.

Realization of aloneness & ownership
     of shame roll down slowly as a collision
         in real time—out of daily, out of context—
the accident victim luxuriously observing
     as in a dream, until (finally!) a bright globe-light
         snaps on overhead,
               the car hits the tree.

I screamed as loudly
     as I could (& never have again); each breath
burst my body, kept climbing:
              water or wind or fire,
     my entire being, crescendo & crash.

    Locked front door, old plates, watercolors,
the wailing—surrounding me—now chosen & *mine*.

Along the Narrow Road Some Sunlight

When the flower shop door jangles the women behind the counter glance up
together, six of them all working in sync & laughing amidst the waiting piles
of roses & gerbera daisies. Their shop feels like somebody's kitchen after
the screen door has banged & they say oh it's you, friend. Come in. Leave
the biting wind outside. Sometimes to write the right words to give with
flowers is difficult. The mourners rip up scratched out cards & start their
messages over again. They try so hard to get it right. Remember Monet in
Paris after the war bringing his waterlilies to the French? In L'Orangerie's big
oval rooms, floor to ceiling *Nympheas* surround the public in an aquarium
of flowers and water. Outside the museum walls lie gray gravel paths &
espaliered fruit trees, granite-blue Seine slipping under the bridges :: inside,
Parisians weary from the ghastly war, so many sons & fathers dead in the
trenches & the fields, walked into cerise & lemon-colored lily blossoms,
no borders, water-light. To enter the gallery, one is instructed to stand in
a portal room then step forward with peace. Today in L'Orangerie tourists
with selfie sticks cruise the rooms everyone taking their own little movies
but in the crowd a man who has traveled many thousand miles just to be
there might start crying loudly with the paintings around him & instead of
shushing him the other patrons pull out their handkerchiefs & blot their
eyes in agreement & weep bewildered together among shimmering blooms.
Cut loose in time. Back in the flower shop a song from long ago plays over
the sound system & all

the flower women
sing along raising their heads
to us in greeting

Remembering Paris

The diphthong rosette is just one rosette
    on a high-ceilinged palm tree (the whole bulk used to be a national mirage).
        We're eavesdroppers,

out for a fandango luncheon on vaccine, so happy.
    I lumberjack in here, not just with retakes but with parodies where I rustle
        every moment.

Inside us strings w/small carcinogens—
    a held-togetherness of lighter explosions. Outside beautiful woods climate
        quickly. Women walk

on cobblestones, their half-lives billowing, their scarves
    & half-lives billowing. The finesse of presumption. I think our best dreams
        are those few

we remember w/o pictures or prompt,
    just talking, when my wilderness asks me what did we manifest there
        again? Oh that's

right, it was packages of jewels
    on our plates. Yes, we had the ozone layer w/ sanctuary, cool on warm,
        like remembering.

Hotel Ljubljana

My secret curls like a miniature finial from a Dragon Bridge lamp.
At night the wind blows through the hotel window, slapping
the scratchy mesh curtain, and I listen to you sleep.

I carry my secret around with us like a bead in tissue; it floats
beyond my fingers in an inner pocket of my blue rain jacket
as we climb gravel paths up the hill to tour the castle.

When I try to feed my secret to sparrows by the open pizza kitchen,
feisty ones flitter behind me at the sound of your shutter. My outline glows
there against the afternoon gloom. This secret is a tiny refusal

—words so difficult they stay impossibly small. River lights blink
through agitated branches. Fiats hiss on drizzly Slovenska cesta
—and a muse leans down to whisper into Prešeren's waiting ear.

When a wedding party strolls out from the castle,
so does a hired Tyrolean band, oompah-pah-ing along the pathways
in the rain. We watch the couple turn to face the cameras of their friends.

Hotel Box with Vermeer Detail, Joseph Cornell, 1955

Every morning his thoughts register surroundings upon waking, same walls that house his body, harbor his soul's ship. His traveler spirit returns. Dream-scraps like seeds & where do they grow? Working on the boxes he moves unmoored drifting like breath while outside finches pass the night huddled against the spine of the arborvitae tossed a little by the sleet.
How these pieces fit together rearranging memory. Cornell the artist loves romance. His entire life sleeps alone at home. Cornell never boards a ship never crosses the Atlantic but never mind; he gathers film stills & magazine clippings, Dutch painting prints & junk shop Grand Tour mementos. Some nights his boxes blue themselves with sand. Each hotel box a dream from a lost century. Open the door. Vermeer's blue-turbaned woman stands by the window her gaze caught as she shifts her weight & her famous pearl earring propels forward the light

only a whisper
from an old Delft street
no one else awake

Hotel Santa Maria

    Two visitors promenade arm-in-arm
on Istiklal Caddesi, wall-to-wall pedestrians at all hours;
        the street sweeps them into the human river pulsing

    north and south and they do not stop
to drink at a café or to shop. They pass the Santa Maria
        three times without seeing it. A gate on the street

    shields the huge staircase leading away,
descending into stone-lined gardens. One finally makes her way
        through the huge iron gate to the top of those big stairs,

    begins to breathe more slowly. Milling crowds
above, music, hawkers, languages buzzing, draw her inward.
        She stands in the air, exhales—her friend wanders

    down the block. The Virgin Mary
mosaic on the church front zooms enormous and faraway
        simultaneously, trick of the stairway's foreshortening.

    To enter here is to open another city, a secret
declension. Other buildings line a widening path to the plaza.
        Santa Maria's façade, four stories high, set back and down,

    rises like a cliff. We stumble
into mysteries, whole universes spinning, that never require us.
        Does the dream really end upon waking? And the door?

Villa Romana Balaca

    Spring brings wind and water to the ruined gardens
of Pannonia, fruit tree boughs toss across
        gravel orchard paths as if wildly
     dancing, offering armfuls of swirling sleeves
to the ghost-villa guests.   Doves chuckle
    above a rock tracery; chambers
  drawn deep into the grass, bones
revealing a millennium.   Time glides unbroken
    where once
  robed women gathered downed branches
from the walkways.   Sage bushes still bloom
    a very pale shade of purple.
They painted these walls with stylized plants,
beautiful lizards, birds, plums;
     patches constellate the plaster like love letters
  scripted on wet paper,
still sticking where thrown so long ago.

     Someone carefully pressed tiny fragments of tile
  into the shapes of nature.   Bees sing
their busy questions zipping flight-lines
    over the warm stones:
How long will you stay this time, human?
Did you make your art to mark your tomb?

Hotel Istanbul

    Cats sleep by the graves;
cats sleep in the park.
        Cats sleep on the sleeping merchant's velvet
    dropcloth in the Sahaflar Carsisi.

In the corners between stone walls and gates cluster
        plastic dishes of cat food and tubs of water.

    Rosewater pudding in a foil cup:
cooked grain, almonds, pistachios,
        golden sultanas, coconut.

    If you are cold, sit by the brazier.
If you are cold, wrap your hands around your teacup.
        If you are cold, lie on a bench in the sun.

    Walk past the old prison.
Walk past Hagia Sophia, Hippodrome, Blue Mosque.
        Walk past the dead under their toppled stones,
the gray dog dreaming, the two-story dessert café.

Turn, gulls above the minarets.
        Turn, ravens on a railing.

    Past chestnut roasters and corn cob vendors.
Past the pomegranate juicers.
        Past the cats curled on a pile of rugs.

Past a man whose back they are loading with boxes.
Past the strait, past the sea.

Every panel of every vista brilliant.
What is it,
what is it you want?

No Reservations

Macao, 2011

The crew films Anthony Bourdain bungee-
jumping
off Macao Tower
into the smog

Footage of Bourdain being suited up
& strapped into the harness
narration backed by guitar jams

I really don't like high places

He says *the hard part isn't looking down*
the hard part is the shaky metal walkway
you've got to creep out on

Previous episodes this season
he has been drinking heavily:
Death Valley, Vienna, Havana,
Haiti, Napoli

Every morning sweating
the filming
until he can start cocktails
at lunch

with whomever: chef friends,
movie stars, local guides

Side-eye at the camera
let's do it

The crew shouts
5
4
3
2
1

Voiceover as his body falls:
then you drop
face forward into space

& for 6 long seconds
but strangely not long enough

you're swimming into air
& life don't hurt anymore

I Think of God in the Turbulence

I think of God in the airplane bathroom with the door that doesn't
close correctly. Thinking in that quavering mirror-light of my reflected
spectral face, my always-exhausted face, of the waste-water receptacles
somewhere under the shaking slippery floor, holding myself so carefully,
those limited movements.

> My first week in a new job a student died & I went with the dean to the
> funeral home to meet the boy's family. I stayed in the dark visitation room
> so long I think anything could have happened, the spirit, flying, flown.

I think of God when others are praying.

> I think of God with my elbows pinned to my sides, when drinking the hot
> tea which I read somewhere is made with unpotable water.

Who cares for me recumbent in those rows of glowing screens each
little screen like a little god, wind screaming unheard outside beyond
the tiny oval windows?

> I was shopping in a market in Hungary when a security guard was sent
> over to tell me there was a bomb scare & the store was being evacuated.
> He was the only one who knew any English. He kept repeating boom
> boom, you must get out.

Does the person next to me think of God? Do they look around & think
that mine might be the last face they see in life?

        I want to push my thoughts into the pilot's brain, as we fly into the sunrise over Greenland, though of course, I cannot.

The Hungarian term for Watch Out (Vygázz!) was always my favorite because of all those dangerous-looking letters. An onomatopoeia for sure but what do we call words that *look* like what they mean? & the way my friend Joe said the Hungarian word *ember*, meaning human, slowly, a blessing in his voice.

Hotel Budapest

Szt István's mummified forearm is not on display,
                                                                 but a golden ceiling
strikes the afternoon dusty light down the touristed apse
     and out the door over the cobbled square in front of his Basilica.

                                            The bathroom in the coffeehouse
across the street requires the code printed on my receipt, crumpled in the garbage.

The market sits on Vamhaz Korut but we miss the market;

       I do not buy anything in Budapest except museum tickets,
passes to a concert in Matyas Church
            and a dish of ice cream.

Szt Iztván is everywhere;
                         his statue gazes stonily back at the Cave Church
which we do not pay to get into by the famous baths we do not pay to get into.

     A lion on Széchenyi Lánchíd turns his exhaust-stained back to me
by a pile of urine-soaked cardboard. Old everything written on by new.

The old everything hanging onto the banks of the Danube for dear life.

        Once this *was* a dear life probably but time is relentless,
buildings over-heated and a wine festival raging on the museum lawn,
            folk dancers flying in circles across a makeshift stage.

Each decision I make feels like a mistake so jet-lagged
the money in my wallet could be lettuce
    because how can something ever cost 12,000 of anything?

Budapest curls its tail around its nose and settles into evening;
the jazz club bolted shut.
                      All those beautiful jewel-box galleries fading
like a big tired fish finally caught with the memories of the ballrooms
he travelled through under-water, who can say that is not so?

                      The splendid chambers
gone forever. I want to sit in a ruined museum-palace doorway,
slouch in the guard's black plastic chair and stare at the same mediocre
El Greco until the light is gone.
                  The kitchens will be closed early
but we can drink together at a little table on Szentharomsag for as long as we want.

After Reading Bashō, I Remember the Rain

I found a quail's nest under sage plants near the house
        woven, I think, while we were traveling,
    & the yard seemed abandoned.

The hen burst out under a torrent of hose-water
        I unknowingly sprayed into the leaves.
    Twelve perfect eggs!

Then days later beneath the variegated branches,
        only shells. Small, each neatly broken
    in half. I spied the button-topped

babies ebbing & flowing after their parents
        ranging through neighborhood, slalom-
    ing arborvitae hedges, half-flying to shrubs,

in the waste-water ditch overgrowth, not back
        to us. So many eggs someone once told me
    because birds are low on the food chain

but that is no comfort. When my mother was dying
        in a hospice far away I was told to come quickly.
    Bad weather closed airports down the coast

rental cars gone & I slept on a bench in Port Authority
        until a train finally delivered me on the day of her death,
    brother and father waiting on a rainy platform.

The living go on living; we visit the rooms of the dying,
        one after another. My father, my dear old father,
    did not survive & like Bashō, he was tired at the end.

Tell me if we return to each other somehow. In bird song? Memory.
        We waited for weeks for the quail to come back,
    walking softly over the gravel by the nest.

Waltham Field Station

Massachusetts Agricultural Experiment, 1948

Squash borers collapse the stems'
long green tracheae inward
like bombed hallways or worn-out veins.

After the count, Jacob snips the borers in half.
Knees of his workpants bow outward
stiff with dirt.

True damage is risked early
in young vines with no secondary roots.
Whit counted 14 borers in a single *Warren Turban* stem—

a record a few years back—but they conclude
thick-stalked plants can harbor
invasion and survive.

Whit's son contracted malaria
in Korea on his 20th birthday,
woke up in a troop ship half-way home.

Longfellow, Alagold, Golden Cushaw
withstand infestation better than
Table Queen, Scallop, Early Prolific—

Jacob and Whit craft the charts,
count larvae under hot August sun.
Whit writes, *Many believed the injury serious*
but we find it much less so.

Hotel Poem

        I sat up sleepless one northern
winter in an old padded armchair
        too fear-choked to rest but nothing

        in fact lurked outside except a wide
shallow river lining a rural route,
        animal trails, and farms. Once

        a gaggle of green-headed turkeys
pooled around my iced-over
        picnic table beeping like TV Martians

        in the yard. I was alone,
yes. Young. When I lay on my side
        something fleeting sometimes

        blocked the light. My thoughts flew
peripherally, penciled escaping kites.
        Cold mornings I'd blink in the sunshine

        mumbling *I'm sorry* to my memories.
Of course the years must pace
        that echoing corridor, lift each glass cover

        from collection trays of rare insects
dead decades now. Is it my work
        to keep watch, dust the high bell jars

       under which the descendants
of pink-and-white lab mice
    nap through the afternoons?

    I live far from the dark mountain
house now; I take drugs at bedtime.
    Vines reclaim framed embroideries

    on the library wall. A ring holds keys
shaped like flattened stars. Maybe
    I let myself sleep because you breathe

    like a sea on the next pillow,
your boy-face unhaunted,
    exhausted.   *Easy now.*

    Leather-bound notebooks
scripted with care lose their deckled-
    edges to decay,

but the years do not read.
    They walk barefoot room after room.

III. DREAMS

Meaning All Meaning Ending Here

there's a way the crash
    of a boisterous river scoring the air above itself

      stops

            completely

when the trail bends into a grove of trees
    and the air hangs blank and clean

    for a second for three seconds five total-nothing

      roaring world suddenly still as
            still as what?

    space that feels like a living animal
        beating-blood breathing surrounded with its own beingness
then *not* anymore

      but where? *how?*

      so much noise
    up-ended (over there by the alders)

Augury

hold her waist so her head can hang
      into the mouth of the well backward
down in the cool exhalation of stone-water

      her mother's hand mirror tipped behind
reflects the pattern a sunlight bargello
      on the oily surface the image of a man

like a black smudge in the snow she sees
      him exactly black crow shot cloudward
above the frozen un-named path

Greenland, 1350

Margret pulls red threads of silk
back from the cloth, spindle whorl
spinning all a spring night half-light—
threads unraveled to sew her new dress.

Then beneath her gray wadmal cloak
she wears a red heart's secret swish & sway.
She whispers wishes to the caged larks
while sweeping the storehouse.

Just last summer alone on strong legs
she hiked up to the sheep pastures &
felt no aches of age—as if she were a girl
again afloat in a sea of sun-warm grass
with no one watching, unsurprised by ghosts.

So quietly the space between worlds stretches
thinner & severs & breathes.

Pratzen Hill

(Acrostic Braid for Robert Duncan & Leo Tolstoy)

Often without warning
I think of Prince Andrei Bolkonsky lying on the battlefield &
am thrown into memory & through memory am
permitted into the high blueness of continual sky
to imagine what he saw while wounded &
return there to stillness
to his desire to rejoin the living.

The room where my father recovered from pneumonia was his
meadow was Austerlitz
as he lay there looking up & inward.
If the Golf Channel played all day in the background
it did not matter. Those greens & whispers
were of the busy confluence of an outside world.

A field near to the heart unspools
scene after scene
made-up & folded in all thought. From his bed my father says
by spring he will walk again. His blue eyes my sky.
The Prince lay wounded while Napoleon rode by inspecting casualties &
mind you, was not dead & moved & moaned & was lifted.

Inscription Found on a Cliff Face After Drought

We fled our valley after the vine-beans withered,
    followed the stream's dwindling trickle to the high trail.

        Burning brushfires chased us up to the treeline, great
flame-bombs leapt grove to dead grove.

The old people used to say to break a drought
    one had to track the tiger,   follow her far

        into the mountains, and wait. Our wasteful lives
caused the water to dry up; our only hope her forgiveness.

We hid in dry weeds for days near her paw marks.
    We offered her our hunger-gifts. She slipped behind rock

    after rock, shy, then radiant. She breathed out dark clouds.
We sang our songs so her tail waved with pleasure, she heard

this story and her sweeping tail raised the rain.   Then we
crossed under marigold gate alive,
                wet petals on our sleeves.

Snowberry in Drought Season

Chinook winds dry out the eastern
    slopes of the Cascades. Snowberry

        thickets' pale pink flowers give over
    in August to bone-white berries.

Good full brush stays green for
    deer, elk & big horns. Black bears

        browse the berries. Drought season
    is a hard season after a hard season

& a hard one again. Snowberry
    lives, rain-less, wind-battered, no matter.

        Grouse, quail & thrushes in their arms.
    Gophers chew root stems in the dark;

rabbits sleep curled underneath
    burrowed all winter. Snowberry

        holds up hillsides in their root nets,
    thick catch-all webs covering

abandoned land. Devastation & ruins from
    old mines taken back. Even burned, snowberry

                    revives with a little sleet-melt.
            Seeds cracked, seeds spread

by birds up & down the dry eastern slopes.

Trail

when I trained I used to run farther & faster than my husband
    & he'd drop me at a high trailhead then drive on to another spot
        & run back toward me   we'd meet in two three four hours

meaning I was mostly on my own from Snoqualmie Tunnel
    to the Rattlesnake parking lot   from Annette Lake
        to North Bend with my hydro-pack & my electrolyte chews

my wad of toilet paper just in case   cell phones didn't work out there
    & I'd keep moving along to the rendezvous   we would start
        early on summer mornings to beat the hikers & I chose hard paths up

the trail was wide open   especially on the back end of the tunnels
    no one   except maybe some Seattle mountain bikers pumping
        in time & intent on their task   I ran the old railbed high above

the highway all morning   ridge on the watershed   micro-climates
    shearing into yet another fern-filled stream-feeder under the undergrowth
        rock croppings in dead grass   trestle bridges swaying with weight

of my footfalls my breathing loud in my head   I saw a young bear on
    a valleyward slope of fieldflowers, light brown & upwind   remembered
        what they say about young bears never without their mothers somewhere

nearby & I thought I should not run toward him   felt like *him* not her
    & I should definitely not run between him & the forest bordering the trail
        so I stood blood pounding in the insect-droned breeze stilling my breath

as he browsed on the hillside   maybe half an hour then kind of tossed
       his head & loped away leaving everything there without him   me
              thinking of his mother still me running down the trail inside of my body

wary for movement in the groundcover   turning the scene
     over my heart again & again   past the old snow sheds & road
            crossings through red cedar groves crunching over leaf-blanketed dirt

with lungfuls of sun-shade spiced air   with that fragrance & heat
     I began this poem   in praise of the red cedar whose scent
            brings those mountain runs back   the trail & young bear

Animate Objects

Whose face changed.
    Whose shoulder worn a groove.
        Whose careful thought.

    Whose cat a boy pharaoh on a blanket.
Whose father in rehab wears torn pants.
    Whose mother no longer.

Whose solitude leaf-blown, matted with rain.
    Whose breeze carries whinnying from the fields.
Whose chives bloom purple mandalas.

      Whose offerings burn from long ago.
Whose hope a foundling on the road.
    Whose ghosts haunt no house.

Whose knives dull.
    Whose secrets frayed hems.
        Whose heart a wretch awake.

Love Poem for Anna Karenina

I hope my copy of *Anna Karenina* is in my COVID-19-abandoned office
But a triathlete dentist in Idaho I once dated might have it.

    That line is telling! Of what, I am not sure exactly. He was fond
Of inserting pop-psych platitudes into our conversations.

His assertion was that I wanted to change him from the self-
    Actualized male human he was. Indeed, reader, I had goals.

Mea culpa, mea maxima culpa. He explained that he was a Martian
& I, as a Venusian, could not apprehend this difficulty.

    I had just moved myself cross-country to a small college town.
Lonely, I reached for his nervous Dalmatian & hard cyclist's thighs.

He flew us to Hawaii for vacation where he asked me to run ahead
    On a cliffside trail so I could turn back to photograph him hiking.

My backpack sagged with his camera equipment. All that money.
I thought the rough sex was fun for a while until it began to feel like hate.

    He said you should read this book by John Gray! Then we can talk!
So I did. In about an hour. Plus a bonus book

He'd recommended—the one about the four agreements.
    (Oh Anna, the things we do when we're starved for love.)

I remember sitting under the trees on his summer-lush lawn at a loss.
He was schooling me from his camp chair. I was his guest.

I'd read his books already, even so I struck a bargain. I said yes, but
Only if you read a book for me. By Leo Tolstoy. It's about relationships.

This from *Anna Karenina*—*I often think that men don't understand what is noble
and what is ignorant, though they always talk about it*—yes, they do, yes.

Cypher

A secret message. The key to a secret message and also one
     having no influence or value; a nonentity
or a design consisting of interwoven letters; a mono-

     gram (which is not an artist's monograph though
those are sometimes hard to decipher). From empty.
     The key to a secret message and also

this cryptographic system in which units of plain old
     text of regular length, usually letters, are arbitrarily
designed and interwoven, mono-

     grams in the transposition of predetermined code or
substituted to form cryptic writing accordingly.
     Where's the message? It's a secret, and also

a defect in an organ resulting in the continuous ohhh
     of a pipe, even when no one has depressed the key.
My design consists of interwoven letters, a mono-

     tone page of graphite under which is written a zero,
from the Old French *cifre*, beautiful arithmetically,
     designed with interwoven letters, rows of dominos: a
secret message. The key to a secret message and so.

National Zoo, January 6, 2021

Xiao Ji Qi, the sleeping panda cub at the zoo, curls himself
into a furry bass clef sign, two black round ears, dots on white.

YouTube videos daily, grainily, carry us into the cage-den,
or out on the rock enclosure where the bamboo is piled up.

A YouTube poster, DoxieMom, warns against negative comments,
notes she is not on the Smithsonian or zoo staff, titles the videos.

Pandas born in the zoo are given Chinese names because their
lives are on loan from China. Xiao Ji Qi translates as Little Miracle,

Little Miracle born to the oldest Giant Panda mother in the US,
her fourth cub. Little Miracle from Mei Xiang, Beautiful Fragrance.

Mei Xiang's three other cubs were sent to China. Her mate Tian Tian
wanders the outside yard. His frozen sperm inseminated Mei Xiang.

Mei Xiang jaws the cub up by the neck or the butt & swiffers him
across the floor to move him. Everything precious hangs by a thread.

Wild Giant Pandas spend their days in trees in China's misty
forests with no enemies except man & environmental destruction.

Xiao Ji Qi rolls into the hollow under Mei Xiang's chin
as they nap; he squeaks & barks at something in his dream.

The American president blamed China for the virus & golfed
while the people died. He sits watching the riots on television.

Number Spell to Change Your Luck

five baby mice in their paper-scrap nest
for many avenues open

four bedposts carved from cedar & polished to shining
for every hotel guest

three berries of blue, purple & green
for sweetness through the hours

both a cat crossing the road & an old man breathing easily all night
for swift feet and no bad dreams

one forsythia bush newly leafed after the drought
for staying long alive.

Daily, Under My Breath

when my husband leaves
the house I wing a small charm
after him in a language

I learned & relearned:
La terre est très belle.
    Mon amour, ici avec toi.

Do the dead press against
the living like wind
billowing a shower curtain

like the warm ghost-weight
of a sleeping pet on the pillow
after they depart?

Do they visit this way?
Like that?
Or as a scrub willow

breaking its branches all
night against the siding scraping
out a message—

    The earth is very beautiful.
My love, here with you.

Was it just last week
we were hiking through a meadow
carpeted in lupine?

Please, may we be lucky.

Not Today

During the pandemic I dream of a cold
baby stuck high in some tree limbs &
I try to catch him then call *help* instead

knee-deep in a snowy field. My hands
stretch forward clumsily like ice gloves &
clouds flee the sky overhead.

When I wake I'm no one, night-blind.
I call one husband's name &
the other catches me instead.

America, there's tea in the ship-holds.
America, tea in your harbor &
America, whose souls hover overhead?

The title of this poem at first read
Nothing. Nothing, all dials spun &
bitter wind catching our clothes instead.

What do we say to the god of death? My friend
visits as a fluttering of curtains, lift &
laugh of a thrush overhead,
rose-branch catching the sun instead.

I Keep the Calendar Alive

with daily treks. A small hawk treads air hunting
then wafts over my head to perch on a pole.

I run in the cold morning past a knot of confused
cattle newly trucked-in to pasture. I yell, *hi cows,*

hi cows. Every one of us breathing, chests up
chests down. They bawl, some tripping, circling

back around. With each step I move myself inside
myself, face pricked by the bright wind bowling

down from the foothills. Our days erode the dream
we thought was time. I am we here as I run alone

along a little used road north of town. Sometimes
I see snakes & skunks. Dead. Alive. Blooms

of gnats catch my hair. Hawk wheeling. That we all die
used to be an abstraction—I count backwards. We. *I.*

After Apple-Picking

Three time zones between us:
early darkness and your early dinners—

you're lining up with the others at 4:45.
I'm in my early afternoon meeting;

I hope your ribs are healing from the fall you
took before Thanksgiving. I know

each day you just try to button your pants or
walk in a straight line or get to the phone

in time to answer it. The person on the
other end is asking you for money

& you can hardly hear her anyway:
a charity, some PAC, that insurance

rep, talking too fast to be understood
by a 92-year-old man going deaf. So

you repeat *I can't understand you* & hang up.
Sometimes your mouth won't form words;

sometimes you forget to get into the bed
& you sleep on top of the covers, cold.

Hard to even look at the calendar
when the days slam down all the same:

hard to get up & hard to stand. I bend
my head to the vision of my father,

a young man running beside my bike,
& before that, the younger man strolling

in Boston, handsome as a candidate,
wearing loafers, cigarette in hand.

The Details

For a while in Paris every woman wore your face
        & I began to believe in the fluidity of time
so all those sharp cheek-boned women were you
    as I watched their progress
down the boulevard or on a run in a park
        or the cant of their hip in front of a painting.

If our what-ever-it-was is over
        I'm sorry. I am only myself. I have sadness
enough for this lifetime & then some.
    Add this to the myriad mysteries I am not equipped
to plumb. The details are impossible, like a dream-
        scrap or the color of the sea.

You are right that I persist in loving the world,
        including you, who dropped into my life
by chance & circumstance & whose elemental
    force is crystalline, serious. As the poets die
I wish we could remember together how we spoke of them
        & read aloud from their books

how we sat up awake with our cigarettes
        someplace perhaps unrecognizable, lost
or destroyed—but that's far beyond us now.

Poem for the Day the World Will End

A bird lands on the arm of the chair outside very close to the window.

Three tiny tangerines & a pomegranate to eat.

My father is alive on this page.

I do not want to be anyone or anywhere else.

I lean over tea in the lamplight with my big book open.

Acknowledgments

Some of these poems have appeared in the following journals and websites, sometimes in different versions or with different titles:

"Animate Objects" in *Sweet: A Literary Confection of Poetry and Creative Nonfiction*

"Augury," "Losers," "Meaning All Meaning Ending Here," and "On the Narrow Road Some Sunlight" in Terrain.org

"After Reading Bashō, I Remember the Rain" and "Crossing to Friday Harbor" in *On The Seawall*

"Cypher" in *The Gettysburg Review*

"Flame in a Jar" and "I Keep the Calendar Alive" in *Bennington Review*

"Hotel Ljubljana" in *The Human*

"Hotel Poem," "Hotel Istanbul," "Hotel Budapest," and "Villa Romana Balaca" in *Green Mountains Review*

"Hotel Vienna" in *Guesthouse*

"Lines for Mid-Winter" in *Fire on Her Tongue: An Anthology of Contemporary Women's Poetry*

"Mercy" in *Tupelo Quarterly*

"Murder Mystery" and "Sleepless Ode" in *Poetry Northwest*

"Snowberry in Drought Season" in *Cascadia: A Field Guide Through Art, Ecology, and Poetry*

"Winter Saturday" in *Washington 129*

"Winter Weather" in *EcoTheo Review*

With Gratitude

Reader, thank you for spending time with my poems. They were written for you.

I am grateful to my students for their trust and for sharing their journeys with me.

Many profound thanks to my super-hero writing group: Sylvia Pollack, Tim Kelly, Kathleen Flenniken, Peter Pereira, Elizabeth Austen, Jared Leising, Diane Aprile, and Jeremy Voigt. What an honor it has been to share poems over the years.

Such gratitude to my friends, colleagues, and fellow writers for their reading, listening, and support: Mark Wunderlich, Julie Olsen, Taneum Bambrick, Maya Jewell Zeller, Xavier Cavazos, Michael Johnson, Lene Pedersen, Anne Bushnell, Judy Hennessy, and Jesse Lee Kercheval.

I am profoundly grateful to Arthur Sze for his generosity.

These judges, editors, and readers extraordinaire gave these poems space and audience: Allen Braden, Derek Sheffield, Simmons Buntin, Ron Slate, Mark Drew, Michael Dumanis, Katherine Riegel, Elizabeth A. I. Powell, Jane Huffman, Diane Seuss, Kelli Russell Agodon, Annette Spaulding-Convy, Major Jackson, Kristina Marie Darling, CMarie Fuhrman, Elizabeth Bradfield, Tod Marshall, Sharma Shields, Crystal Brandt, and Keetje Kuipers.

Thank you to Elaina Ellis for her excellent advice on this manuscript.

Many thanks to Alain Brichau at La Muse Writers' and Artists' Retreat, Steve Silber, Alice Pettway, Mara Bartlett Asenjo, and the whole crew at the Chutlitna Lodge Resident Artist Program, all of the fantastic people at Virginia Center for Creative Arts, Danielle Epstein at the Marble House Project, and Central Washington University for time, space and invaluable support.

Shout out to Alliance Française and Institut de Français for helping me grapple with French.

Deep appreciation to Kevin Craft, Kary Wayson, and Abi Pollokoff at the Possession Sound Series for Poetry NW Editions. I could not be happier.

This book is given in memory of my father, Richard Owens Whitcomb, whose love I feel ongoing.

And, Larry Varin, you are my home.

Notes on the Poems

Epigraphs: The Maggie Nelson quotation is from her iconic poetry collection *Bluets*, in which the artist Joseph Cornell's life, art, and use of the color blue is featured and examined.

      The Deborah Digges quotation is from her poem "the wind blows through the doors of my heart" in her posthumous poetry collection of the same name.

"Losers," with its litany of losses, orbits around Elizabeth Bishop's famous poem, "One Art." My favorite Aimee Bender story, described in this poem, is "Loser" in her collection *The Girl in the Flammable Skirt*.

"Crossing to Friday Harbor" is in conversation directly with Walt Whitman's poem, "Crossing Brooklyn Ferry." The Friday Harbor in my title is located on San Juan Island in Washington State.

"Sestina of Human Longing" references a Stanley Plumly poem in its third stanza. That wonderful poem is "Doves in January" from Plumly's collection *Now That My Father Lies Down Beside Me: New & Selected Poems*.

"Meaning . . . all meaning ending here" is a line spoken by Povel Wallander, Kurt Wallander's father, in the BBC TV series *Wallander*, Season 2, Episode 3, "The Fifth Woman."

"Augury" describes a scene from the novel *Cold Mountain* by Charles Frazier and the film based on the novel, directed by Anthony Minghella.

"Greenland, 1350" is written about a character in Jane Smiley's novel *The Greenlanders*, and is for Mark Wunderlich.

"Pratzen Hill" references a scene in Leo Tolstoy's *War & Peace* set during the Battle of Austerlitz in the Napoleonic Wars. The first words of each line read in sequence form the opening line of Robert Duncan's poem "Often I Am Permitted to Return to the Meadow."

"Inscription Found on a Cliff Face After Drought" was written in response to a print by the artist Anthony Kroes.

Iron Horse State Park Trail in Washington State has been renamed Palouse to Cascades State Park Trail and is an historic rail trail traversing 250 miles east-west. "Trail" describes running on the trail through a section in the Cascade Mountains.

"After Apple-Picking" alludes to the Robert Frost poem of the same title. This poem is dedicated to my father, who is done with apple-picking now.

None of the hotels in the titles and poems in this book are real hotels, except the Hotel Poem in Istanbul.

Photo by Rosanne Olson

Katharine Whitcomb is the author of *Saints of South Dakota & Other Poems*, which won the Bluestem Award, chosen by Lucia Perillo, and *The Daughter's Almanac*, which won the Backwaters Prize, chosen by Patricia Smith. Her chapbook, *Lamp of Letters*, won the Floating Bridge Chapbook Award. She was a Stegner Fellow at Stanford University and is the recipient of fellowships from the Fine Arts Work Center in Provincetown, the Wisconsin Institute for Creative Writing, MacDowell, Yaddo, and elsewhere. She teaches at Central Washington University and divides her time between Washington State and Vermont. More information about the author and her work can be found at www.katharinewhitcomb.com.

POSSESSION SOUND POETRY SERIES

Sierra Nelson, *The Lachrymose Report*

Lauren Hilger, *Morality Play*

Katharine Whitcomb, *Habitats*

Poem text set in Kepler STD with
section breaks in Citrus Gothic Solid
Book design by Abi Pollokoff
Printed on archival quality paper

Poetry NW Editions is an independent, non-profit educational press in residence at Everett Community College.

Founding Editor: Kevin Craft
Managing Editor: Abi Pollokoff

www.ingramcontent.com/pod-product-compliance
Lightning Source LLC
Chambersburg PA
CBHW052121070526
44586CB00016B/2026